POETIC
RAMBLINGS
— OF A —
HOPEFUL
HEART

POETIC RAMBLINGS
OF A
HOPEFUL HEART

SHERYL GRIFFIN

POETIC RAMBLINGS OF A HOPEFUL HEART

iUniverse books may be ordered through booksellers or by contacting:

iUniverse
1663 Liberty Drive
Bloomington, IN 47403
www.iuniverse.com
1-800-Authors (1-800-288-4677)

Because of the dynamic nature of the Internet, any web addresses or links contained in this book may have changed since publication and may no longer be valid. The views expressed in this work are solely those of the author and do not necessarily reflect the views of the publisher, and the publisher hereby disclaims any responsibility for them.

Any people depicted in stock imagery provided by Thinkstock are models, and such images are being used for illustrative purposes only. Certain stock imagery © Thinkstock.

ISBN: 978-1-4917-8876-9 (sc)
ISBN: 978-1-4917-8877-6 (e)

Library of Congress Control Number: 2016916775

Print information available on the last page.

iUniverse rev. date: 10/12/2016

This book was conceived with the intention of sharing the ups and downs of love, and everything in between from a bipolar perspective of intensity.... the dark depressions, the loneliness, the raw emotions, broken hearted disappointments and frustrations to the elation of hope and possibilities. I want this book to make people think, to question their existence, to revitalize their hearts, to dare to dream, to offer the opportunity to believe in love, in yourself and in the higher power that continually lifts us above the pain and misery to show us the possibilities of love.

My heart concedes it has more than once believed in the fairy tale.

This edition of Poetic Ramblings is a compilation of many years and many relationships I have had during my lifetime. I tried to focus on the bittersweet beginnings and the more positive aspects and hope that love can inspire the heart to believe and if all else fails to have the faith and courage to try again.

The books title is a bit complex. Most of these poems came from the pain and devastation when love is lost, but no matter what I have always had hope. The emotional bliss that love provides rarely lasts a lifetime. In our minds we create the myth and only in our dreams and in fairy tales does anyone live happily ever after. But our hearts are foolish and can be easily convinced with each new endeavour that there is such a thing as forever. Sadly, in life only two things are guaranteed .... birth and death..... and you experience them both alone. Therefore, we spend our entire lives searching for another half of something we have had within us the whole time. The journey towards love of self is evident in these pages and imperative for any kind of love to have any chance to survive and thrive.

This book is primarily dedicated to my mother. She was my biggest fan but now she is gone. She watches from heaven as her legacy lives on. I am fulfilling a promise that I made to her, to publish another book, a hopeful ramblings edition. My mother always believed in me especially when my heart was broken and I didn't believe in myself. She taught me what real love is and how to apply it to my life, my relationships and my family.

This book is also dedicated to my amazing children, Samantha and Christopher. They have always been there to pick up the pieces when my heart was shattered and smother me in the only true love I have ever known.

This edition of ramblings of course would not have been possible if it were not for all the people who touched my heart or my life with love. I would be remiss if I didn't thank them all for their love, for lifting me up, letting me down and letting me go. To all those who loved me to death and those who did nothing but lie to me. It inspired the pages of this book and brought me to where I am in my life at this moment. It is my proof and evidence of my hearts resilience and my faith in "once upon a time."

Contents

Possibilities

For every moment in life
There is the possibility
Of a miracle being created
For every time
You risk your heart for love
There is the possibility
You have found "the one"
For every choice you make
As you follow your path
There is the possibility
You will discover your own self worth
For every emotion you feel
That you have the courage to share
There is the possibility
Of finding a true friend who cares
For every mistake
Every pain, every ache
There is the possibility
You will learn and grow
For every action
That requires contemplation
There is the possibility
You will deepen your soul
For every word you speak
Every promise you keep
There is the possibility
To acquire the respect you seek
If every moment, every day
You are grateful in some way
The possibilities
Will become realities

For every moment
Can be magic
You can create
A lifetime of memories
If you have the faith
And believe
In life's possibilities

Authors Comments:
"I wrote this for myself and my children as a reminder to be open to every encounter in life. For every person you meet, every situation you end up in lends itself to the endless possibilities life has to offer if you. You just need to be open minded to the universe and all its wisdom."

I Was Dreaming

I was dreaming
I was writing
Love left waiting
Heart left starving

Deep in a meditation
Far beyond myself
Defying explanation
Perfect body, perfect health

Spirit searching for salvation
Mind hunting for the truth
Body exploring the passion
Lost love, forgotten youth

Running out of air
I feel the sun on my skin
Ravenous and bare
Ready to love again

Awoken from this vision
Conscious of its details
Fantasies fascination
Does true love prevail?

I am calm but breathless
Responsive to the meaning
No longer am I powerless
It's time I start believing

I manage my own future
I can live in abundance
I see the bigger picture
I create my circumstance

I have faith
I am where I need to be
I adore my life
Someday love will find me

Authors Comments:
"I find myself continually trying to remind and re invent myself and the way I look at things to promote change and growth."

You Are

You are my light in the dark
My conscious through the clouds
The voice of reason
In a tornado of doubt

You are the calm in the storm
And the rainbow at the end
You are graceful and warm
You are my best friend

You are the most fragrant flower
In any bouquet
You emanate love and power
Wisdom and strength

You are the bird that sings
To keep my spirit awake
My guardian angel with wings
That guides every step I take

You are the whisper in the wind
That confirms who I am
A tree that grew firm
Yet always knows how to bend

You are the echo in the silence
In a world full of noise
You are a treasure in the ocean
That brings great wealth and joy

You are the ears that listen
With love and concern
To all my confusion
About lessons I must learn

You are the rock that I stand on
In my garden of peace
The one I rely on
For balance and faith

I thank God every day
For the little things in life
That bring me closer to you
And remind me of your love

Authors Comments:

*"This was originally written for my mother, but I get this feeling of gratitude
when I realize all the people who have helped me to feel loved"*

You Say I Hold Your Heart

You say I hold your heart
In the palm of my hand
The truest form of art
Takes years to understand

The most beautiful structures
Took centuries to form
Even the scriptures
Took time to translate and learn

Yet in a matter of days
Lives have been changed
Words written
Hearts saved

Risks taken
Mountains moved
Fear forgotten
Love found
Prayers spoken
Wishing you were around

Graciously I accept
Holding your heart
Spirits connect
Even worlds apart

I will love and protect
Each ounce that you share
Trust and respect
With loyalty and care

I shall not neglect
I will not fear
Whatever comes next
I am here

Authors Comments:
"for Robert"

Believe

Sometimes it's complicated
To believe and have faith
To let go of your fear
To sit silent and wait
To see the unseen
To trust in a higher power

When you can't see the beauty in yourself
You just have to believe
When you lose sight of love
Pain consumes your soul
You have to learn to rise above
And just believe

When you can't see the best
In people or places you know
Think of it as a test
To get to a higher plateau
So you will believe

When you find it hard to forgive
Take a look in the mirror
Learn to live
And believe

When all hope is lost
And you're ready to give up
Let go and trust
The result will amaze
And you will believe

Believe in your dreams
Believe in your power
Believe in your destiny
Believe in your desire

Keep the faith
Keep the questions
Keep looking both ways
Keep the fire and the passion

To feel the strength
To feel the love
All you really need
Is to BELIEVE

Authors Comments:
"Whatever you believe and trust will become what you live"

My Perfect Pets

As my personal therapy
I take a moment each afternoon
To remove the clutter from my mind
Erase the thoughts that consume
Relax and unwind
I lie in the hammock
Peanuts in hand
Watching my furry friends frolic
Dance, fly and land
They jump from the ground
And drop from the trees
Knowing I am around
With their favorite treats
They climb up my legs
Take nuts from my toes
There's no need to beg
I never say no
They dig and scamper
Bury and hoard
One after another
Life is good
They amuse me and please me
Keep a smile on my face
As they look and say "feed me"
My worries are erased
They exercise caution
But know I will do them no harm
They lift my depression
Just racing up my arm
They scurry about
Tails all up and waving
They chatter and shout
They're not into sharing

This play continues
Till the sun starts to set
Goodnight my squirrels
My perfect little pets

Authors Comments:

"I found myself raising four infant squirrels, once upon a time. They were abandoned and no bigger than my thumb. I nurtured and fed them until they were old enough to be set free. And even after I let them go they returned year after year answering to my call. I considered it a very special relationship to have with a wild animal. They are still some of my fondest memories."

Just for You

How many perfect moments
Can you provide
How much effort does it take
To put everything aside

To enjoy the here and now
How often do you think
If I showed you how
With a promise and a wink

Would you want the job
Could I pass on this gift
To turn life into a dream
Would you call it a curse
And run back to make believe

I go out of my way
To see the dream before it starts
Then I take the "time" to play
It comes straight from the heart

There's magic in my memories
Because I put it there
Like the muscles on my arms
Or the blonde in my hair
No instant body
No perfect pill
Simple discipline
And a strong stubborn will

It's hard work
To be special and unique
It's impossible
To do it seven days a week

So we live for the perfect moments
Although they may be few
They were created and spent
JUST FOR YOU

Authors Comments:
*"Every moment you share with someone else is
an opportunity to create a perfect moment"*

Fall

How did I fall into
This amazing place
Too good to be true
An infinite smile on my face

Wrapped in arms
Of love and comfort
Sympathetic and strong
With no effort

How did I fall
So deep and so fast
When my heart was so small
From the pain of the past

Yet I am lost in his eyes
Without hesitation
A trust that defies
Reasonable explanation

A touch I never had
But always craved
A simple man
Himself waiting to be saved

A passion so honest
With all its issues and history
Even the darkest test
Seems to set the spirit free

No more painful bondage
From muddy water or quicksand
At this crucial stage
He still tries to understand

His endeavours are incredible
He is not hindered by a challenge
His heart is loyal
I giggle at his "twinge"

How did I fall into love
On the wings of a prayer
This angel fell from above
And I am so grateful he is here

I don't care how I fell
As long as it is mutual
Scream "hell yea" ring the bell
Comprehensive visual

For A Moment Let's Pretend

For a moment let's pretend
That we are more than friends
Close your eyes and come with me
Into my world of fantasy

Where every day is filled
With happiness and joy
Living out our dreams
No defences to deploy

No anger, no greed
No selfish jealousy
Caring for each other's needs
With no regret or animosity

Mutual pride in what we share
Knowing love is always there
True appreciation
Hard work and determination
Mutual satisfaction
Constant communication

Just imagine if you will
The balance we would feel
With your arms around me tight
Sleeping next to me each night

Waking to my kisses
On the back of your neck
My gentle caresses
On your shoulders and your back
Sharing in a life
As husband and wife
Sharing a dream
Reaching for a goal
Questioning all we believe
To deepen our minds and our souls

Now open your eyes
Look into mine
I am real ......I am alive
I don't want to waste any more time

From this day I do vow
To be true to how I feel
To speak the truth that I know
To be faithful, to be "real"
To live in the here and now
To be humble, to be true
To give you my heart
To share eternity with you

Love Is Still What I Find

In the interest of being fair
I need you to feel how much I care
I need you to see inside my soul
How your love has burned a perfect hole?
Allowing me to breathe
Making it easier to set you free
Happy to watch you fly
Believing I am the reason why
I see you spread your wings
A million memories flood my mind
Yet after everything
Love is still what I find
I gave you all the love I had
Then I gave a little more
I always held your hand
As you were running out the door
I recall holding each other tight
Even closer after we had a fight
We made each other strong
Even when we weren't getting along
Together we've laughed and cried
Shared our lows and our highs
No challenge I wouldn't try
Knowing you were by my side
I knew then that you would leave
I still handed you my heart
I love you unconditionally
No regrets ...... no remorse
For now, I'll let you go
To soar among the stars
I need you to know
My love is never far

So close your eyes and breathe
And dream of possibilities
Life gives no guarantees
So I take your love with me

Authors Comments:
*"I wrote this for my babies, who are now adults and finding out who they want
to be..... Sometimes it is so hard to love so deeply only to set them free"*

You Saw the Beauty

You didn't just look at me
To see the attractive skin
You didn't look past me
Or notice what I was wearing

You saw the beauty
Of who I am within
The dynamic energy
Of who I am becoming
From where I have been

In a glance you established
I'm on the correct path
And then, not by chance
You told me for yourself

As you reached for a hug
And whispered in my ear
Kinetic energy understood
What I never before could hear

"You are beautiful"

I give you my sincerest gratitude
For this gift of confirmation
One brief interlude
You gave me the power of my conviction
Your words took on new meaning
You saw inside .... The power and strength

The passion I hide... for fear of failing
You showed me your belief

In a moment all too fleeting
This positive energy from my source
It was a pleasure meeting
Such an influential force

Authors Comments:
"This one is dedicated to Wayne Dyer who after a symposium of one of his books, he gave me an autograph, a hug and a gift of awareness that I am on the right path"

You Are Heart, I Am Soul

You are heart, I am soul
You go fast, I go slow
We both need love
Not control

Attention, affection
Patience, passion
No need to mention
All the forms of adoration

Friendship is primary
Everything else is a possibility
I know what I see
The same things you see in me

Clueless, hopeless
Cautious, in focus
Simply searching for happiness
In a world full of madness

Peace and serenity
Calm, positive energy
Silence that is golden
Words and thoughts known
But not spoken

Honest communication
Trust with no expectations
Space without questions
Faith in this connection

Love without conditions
Monogamous devotion
Loving protection
Only strengthens the emotion

You are heart
I am soul
A brand new start
I don't plan to let this go

Will you ..... With Me

Will you stand with me
Naked in the mirror
I want to feel the energy
The warmth of her

Will you walk with me
Naked under the moon
Exposing everything
Knowing I will protect you

Will you dance with me
Naked in a field of daisies
Live out your fantasies
Not if … not when … no maybes

Will you catch me when I fall
Teach me to swim
Will you make me call
Or will you *know* where I am

Will you play with me
Barefoot in the puddles
Naked in the pouring rain
Squishing mud between our toes

Will you lay with me
Naked on a beach
The only stars we'll see
Will be within our reach

Will you sleep with me
Naked in my arms
Let me satisfy your need
Let my body keep you warm

Will you catch me when I fall
Teach me to swim
Will you make me call
Or will you *know* where I am

What Would I Give

What would I give
To feel you again
The warmth of your touch
The love between friends

Would I sell my soul
For your sweet caress
My logic says no
But my body screams yes

A gentle embrace
That always meant more
A smile on my face
A kiss at the door

I never knew
What it was that I felt
But I shook in my shoes
And you made my heart melt

Now that I know what it is that I want
I thought I could get it from you
But I'm not willing to sell myself short
I need to know that you want it too

Empty House

I don't know where to begin
I've never done this before
Combining two into one
My heart cannot ignore
The fear and the doubt
From lives twice removed
Trying to figure out
If trust has been proved
Looking around
Disappointment and pain
The echoing sounds
Of silence remain
Feeling emotions
Absorbed in the walls
Years of conditions
Spirits withdrawal
Realities resolution
Like the eye of a storm
Confirms speculation
The magic is gone
Picking up the pieces
Of hope and faith
Filling the spaces
With personal taste
Still starving
Comfort accumulated
Energy building
Love consummated
Still searching
For solutions
Mutually satisfying
Individual passions

Patience
Reprieve
Romance
Believe

Authors Comments:
"This was written after starting a new relationship and seeing the end of one for the beginning of another. We all have a past, baggage that we carry from previous encounters but when it is all said and done we can only hope the new love can cover and exceed anything we have felt before."

Road to Recovery

This road to recovery
Is hard and long
Time to invest in me
Find out where I belong

An amazing discovery
Of what went wrong
Allowing negativity
To break me down

From wishing to be dead
To coming back to life
These demons in my head
Cut me deeper than any knife

Yet here I am breathing
Dealing with the pain
I need to start believing
In miracles again

Love will overcome
All obstacles and distractions
I know I can be strong
Through my recuperation

Once my balance is found
I'll be on my way
No turning around
Love will keep the demons at bay

I will not surrender
Or give up my faith
That there is something better
Waiting for me someday

Authors Comments:
*"So often a heart gets broken and it takes time and perseverance
to heal and know it was all part of the plan"*

To Be Lonely

To be lonely
And to be alone
Are opposites
Seen as the same
One considers those around you
One defines your frame of mind
In your heart
You feel isolated
Too far gone
For a friend
A surface smile illustrated
To prove there is a future
Before the end
To believe
You will be alone
Is to blow out the candle
Before it is lit
Why even bother anymore
You may as well quit
To bounce back from a fall
Takes strength from within
To accept life as it is
Is to build brick after brick
To learn to pretend
And to understand
Just where the wall
Inside your head shall end

Authors Comments:
"And then you find a way to the path that begins toward love again"

Hope

Hope is what comes
After many days of darkness
Sitting right behind faith
Your spirit somehow missed

That burning light within
That guides us through the storm
Even when we are too blind
To sit silent, listen and be calm

The ray of sunshine
That lingers on your face
To remind you that this world
Is not such an awful place

The echo of a child's laughter
When your children are grown
Believing in happily ever after
No matter how much hatred has been shown

Having trust in love
Despite years of being burned
Knowing with every failure
There's a lesson to be learned
Hope springs eternal
With life's possibilities
Love is perpetual
When given unconditionally

In The Middle of My Chaos

In the middle of my chaos
I take time to breathe
In the midst of my confusion
I demand time for me
A little work, a little play
Candles in my corner
At the end of the day
Time has become so precious
I had forgotten how good it feels
To enjoy the fruits of my labour
In the simplest forms
In my children's laughter
My pets, my home
So I take a deep breath
And try to clear my mind
Of all the various lists
That consume my time
I remind myself
How lucky I am
How hard I have worked
To get where I stand
My mind starts to wander
Back to all the things that need to be done
To keep my life together
So I guess it's time to run

My Kayak

My floating orange
Exercise machine
An amazing boost
To my self esteem
The control of muscles
My whole body tingles
As I paddle into each wave
The natural connection
My spirit craves
The meditative motion
The silence and strength
Of the ocean
Soaking in the power
Of the sun's hot rays
Rest for a few
Let the waves carry me
Enjoying the view
Sweet serenity
Ripples of the water
Carry my worries away
No past, no future
Just this moment
This beautiful day

War

Who would you die for
If we were all sent to war??

Who would you save
And what would you pay??

How would you chose
What would you lose??

When your last breath is inhaled
Will you feel like you have failed??

What would you sacrifice
To save someone's life??

Whose hand would you take
If you knew it may break??

When your last tear falls
Will it be known you gave your all??

Whose memory would you honour
If there were no suits of armor??

Whose heart would you chase
If the past could be erased??

When you close your eyes to pray
Do you wish the world would go away??

Whose path would you cross
If you knew what could be lost??

Whose arms and eyes would you fall into
If you knew everything they'd been through??

Whose soul would you hold
Alive or dead??
Young or old??

Authors Comments:
"I wrote this after watching a movie called "four feathers".
It inspired these words"

My Intimate Silent Prayer

My intimate, silent prayer
Would be to thank you
For always being there

For the moments you held me
Tightly in your arms
Or wrapped your spirit around me
To save me from harm

I am grateful for the love
We make and we share
When no one else
Understands or cares

For the quiet whispers
You send with the breeze
Promising we'll be together
One of these days

I am grateful for the hope
To hold you in this world
Yet I would happily let go
And just be your little girl

As a woman I digress
To being slightly obsessed
In things that I miss
In being your mistress

But I am grateful to touch
The fire in your heart
To play with the man I love so much
Even beyond death we shall not part

This simple prayer
Comes with a tear
As I watch you there
And I am here

I will hold steadfast to the pledge
Of a soul that I trust
Be a patient poetess
Despite the obvious

I just want you to know I am yours
Completely
I wait for the days
When we can share that mutually

Puzzle Pieces

Secrets told
Release the soul
From the evil hold
Of demons control

Held inside
They eat away
Destructive pride
Hypocrisy

Painful walls
Pitiful truths
Words that echo
From past abuse

Buried beneath
The surface of the future
Chemicals and colors bleed
To fade the picture

Facts denied
Create the illusion
There's something to hide
Adding to the confusion

Time and space
Put the past to rest
But cannot erase
The negative affects

Love provides
New investments
Souls collide
Hearts contentment

Hope restored
Brings excess profit
Spirit no longer ignored
The puzzle pieces finally fit

Authors Comments:

"Sometimes letting go of the sorrow requires someone to hold you, so you can work through the pain knowing you will never really be alone"

Lost and Disenchanted

How did so many people
Linked through God in spirit
Become so isolated and alone
Disconnected and desperate

When did society decide
The skin is more important
When did the growing soul inside
Become insignificant

When did love become a game
To be used and manipulated
Words spoken in vain
Carelessly articulated
People pretending
To be what they are not
Suspiciously defending
The empty life they've got

What happened to allegiance
Commitment and honesty
Where is the romance
Why is everyone so finicky

So many broken hearts afraid to fail
Lost and disenchanted
Searching for the fairy tale
Forgetting that love is meant
To be unconditional

Missed

It amazes me
The simplicity
Of feeling needed
And being missed
In a moment
When all was lost
I stood silent
Towel tossed
All it took
Was a word
In print
A thought
To bring me back
To here and now
And re connect
Body and soul
Through internet
Or telephone
Energy sent
Suddenly aware
I am not alone
I was missed
I am flattered
And amazed

Authors Comments:
"This is for Richard"

Half of Something

Half of something
That never was
Anything
Except love
Naïve
Blind
To believe
I could find
Half of something
That was
Already whole
Within the soul
Fragile
Weak
Breakable
Admit defeat
Half of something
That turned out to be
Nothing
But agony
Self inflicted
Suicide
Future predicted
Black and white
Half of something
That use to be
Everything
But reality
Silence
Anger
No penance
For a liar
Half of something
I remember
Spirit with wings
Words of forever

Deception
Disgust
Destruction
Of trust
Half of something
Impossible
Everything
Is replaceable
Half of something
New and original
Anything
Is possible

Spirit

The spirit which is told
Holds love deeper than the soul
Then, what is felt to be old
And worth much more than gold

Emotions deep embrace
Not knowing they were chased
Searching for a light
They wander through the night

Yet this spirit strong
No distance too long
Uncontrolled connections
In fear of rejection

Black or white; day or night
Consciously confused
Spirit fly; spirit fight
Angry or amused

To laugh; to cry
The question remains...... why?
If the spirit chose to fly
Would it also choose to die?

Trying

Trying to be strong
Trying to be patient
Sometimes it seems so long
Between messages sent
Trying to understand
Trying to read between the lines
Trying to comprehend
If you are still mine
Trying not to doubt
Or become paranoid
Can't help but to pout
My heart has a void
Trying to be a friend
No expectations
Trust trying to mend
Lost in my passion
Not wanting the chase to end
Trying to get through
Another empty day
Without missing you
Or the way we used to play
Trying to keep the faith
That it will all work out okay
Trying to follow the path
That will reconnect you to me
Trying to be hopeful
Love still exists
Beyond your list of things to do
That I take precedence
Trying harder than I think you know
To keep it together and let love grow

Be A Man

Be a man…..let it go
You know what you need to do
Why hold on to the chains
You're only adding links to the pain

Be a man…..let it slide
You know what you're trying to hide
You're only fooling yourself
With your ego and your pride

Be a man…..cut some slack
If it's real, it will come back
You can't force love into reality
If it's not meant to be

Be a man…. Let it go…. Set it free
Be a man…..stand firm
Let your heart lead the way
Live…. Laugh…. Learn
It's what you DO not what you say

Be a man…..get a life
I'm your friend…..not your wife
Fight your loneliness like the rest of us
Stand up to your fear and kick its ass

Be a man…..get tough
Remember love is never enough
Accept your addictions and control them

Be a man…..stop the lying
To yourself and your friends
You keep saying that you're trying
And you will do anything
But what I see are simply words
No action
Phrases and excuses
You want my recommendation
BE A MAN

Authors Comments:
"Being a good friend can be difficult at times, it is hard to tell a friend your own truth, when you know what they need to hear and what they want to hear are two separate things"

How Sweet It Is

How sweet it is; to be loved by you
To be held so close; to a love so true
How sweet it is; to kiss your lips
Or be caressed; by your fingertips
Sweeter than candy; more bizarre than an orange moon
I love the way you love me; you know I love you too
How sweet it is; to see your smile
Like a summer breeze; or a happy child
How sweet it is; to touch your heart
To feel your love; when we are apart
How sweet it is; to be your friend
Knowing changes will come; the love doesn't end
How sweet it is; that with a simple sigh
You know something's wrong; and you always ask why
Sweeter than candy; more bizarre than an orange moon
I love the way you love me; and you know I love you too
How sweet it is; that you reached out your hand
Not quite sure; that I would understand
How sweet it is; the way you look at me
The way you pick me up; sweep me off my feet
How sweet it is; to feel a love so strong
To feel so secure; how could it be wrong
How sweet it is; that you try so hard
Just to please me; against all the odds
Sweeter than any candy; more bizarre than an orange moon
I love the way you love me; you know I love you too
How sweet it is

Authors Comments:
"For ED"

You Tell Me

You tell me I have not changed
Since the day you met me
That I just refuse to hide my pain
I have not set the demon free

You tell me I sabotage my happiness
Someone must have touched my heart
Determined to end the bliss
The demons do their part

You tell me I am not weak
Yet I cannot get out of bed
I hear the words you speak
Over the pounding in my head

You tell me there is hope
That I do this to myself
Unconsciously I invoke
This demon from his shelf

You tell me to be strong
I push, because I am afraid
Intuitions never wrong
Demon starts to fade

You tell me of your love
As a mentor and a friend
You always show up
An angel in the wind
Thank you again
For all the energy you send

Feed The Fire

Someday you'll want to play with me
When an offer is made
You'll find out how much fun I can be
Without getting laid
Someday you'll feel my energy
When you are alone
In the whisper of the trees
Or the lyrics of a song
Someday I'll be a priority
Something you can't live without
More than air, food or sleep
This is guaranteed without a doubt
Love is a gift
Rare and wonderful
When a spirit is missed
More than a body is comfortable
Someday I hope you acquire
The necessary ambition
To feed my fire
Beyond physical passion
Do not be mistaken
I am grateful
But in the crazy world we live in
I want something more spiritual
A deeper connection
Than just skin
A silent conversation
Where my soul can swim
Someday you'll want to do more than just float
On the surface of a wave
When you jump out of the boat
I want to be the one you crave
Diving deep into the ocean
To talk to the whales and the dolphins
That intimate connection
To all that is.........and ever has been
I want to dance amongst the stars
With you by my side
No matter where we are

Spread your wings and fly
Someday you will know and understand
Why absence makes the heart grow fonder
Despite being a simple man
You will see why magic makes everything better
In the details you will find
Infinite passion and pleasure
And "out of sight, out of mind"
Will be replaced with wanting "forever"
Someday you will see my power
And know who I am
More than a witch, goddess, lover, mother
I am the beginning and the end

Every 28 Days

Every 28 days
We shed our skin
Like a snake
From within

An ancient sacred ritual
Known far and wide
Following the moons cycles
Since the beginning of time

Emotions that run rampant
Mood swings at the drop of a pin
This cursed atonement
Imagined as a sin

Some call us monsters
Evil witches come to mind
Feminine ogres
With a common tie that binds

This gift we were given
To populate the land
Secret pains well hidden
Men will never understand

Wicked monthly traditions
Connect us to our source
Criminal reactions
We are at our worst

Ceremonial darkness
As we bleed to death
New heightened awareness
Virginal and refreshed

There is a conscious knowledge
As the angel reappears
Intuitive balance
The cycles end is near

Authors Comments:
"Being a woman is an amazing process of growth and death that is ever changing and evolving to create the goddesses we become"

Tr7 My Love

I never had an obsession
Quite this strong
With anything
Or anyone
With you it's so different
We each understand
Exactly what
The other demands
No neglect
You won't let me down
I keep you up
You respond
By getting me higher
Than I've ever been
And keeping me there
Every time I get in
With curves so sharp
You turn everyone's eyes
Children, guys, girls
You simply mesmerize
Your silky shine
Reflects my love
Every perfect line in your body
Puts you above all the rest
Makes you stand out in a crowd
And you know how
That makes me proud
Our love is one
That is rare
I know it will endure
Through damage and repair
No matter what the cost
You'll always look your best
Though you show me time and again
It's you who gives the test

I'll pass it each day
As I pass each car on the way
And my love for you
Will never go away

Authors Comments:

"A rare gift is when you love something or someone and have to let them go for one reason or another........ then years later you can recapture the emotions with equal or more intensity.... I have been this lucky"

Lost and Renewed

Here I am
Being selfish again
Thinking no one understands
The pain that I am in

When doubt and confusion
Start to build
All other emotions
Are put on hold

One stupid reaction
Leads to another
Demanding explanations
Of why we are together

Fear consumes
With its theories and questions
Heart becomes tormented
With deeper expectations

Lost in a cycle
Of negativity
Affecting the people
Who mean the most to me

Please accept my sincerest apologies
For dragging you into my insanity
Thank you for your honesty
And for speaking your truth with such integrity

I had forgotten how easily
I become devoured
By my own hypocrisy
Feeling unloved and overpowered

Believing I am unworthy
I become a coward
Unbalanced and unhappy
Because I didn't feel needed

Yet in your love and simplicity
You shared your opinion
Making me feel silly
About my self examination

You reminded me
The story has two sides
It's difficult to see
When I run away and hide

No one said love was easy
Sensitivity goes both ways
That with my depressive energy
I am impossible to please

With your love and loyalty
I am ready to accept
Responsibility
For my own neglect

Time for me to wake up
And be grateful
Time for me to stop
Acting pitiful

I am making this my new years resolution

To try harder to maintain a positive attitude
To increase my motivation
To fall deeper in love with you
To do everything with passion

To recognize my faults
Acknowledge my dysfunctions
Yet refusing to self destruct
But continue my explorations

To invest time and magic
Where it will be returned
For mutual benefits
Of all those concerned

To live every day
With the power of my convictions
To inspire my spirit to play
Without boundaries or conditions

To express my poetic thoughts on paper
Without fear of rejection
To practice the things that give me pleasure
Aware I cannot achieve perfection

To keep reminding myself
I am where I need to be
Karma works and life is good
I create my own destiny

Always hoping for the future to be better
But satisfied where I am
Content in knowing we are together
And you are my man

Authors Comments:
*"This was written as an affirmation and a resolution to try and prompt
my brain to focus on who I am and where I want to be."*

Mystery Sublime

All these long years I was searching for a prince
When I should have been looking for a knight
Lonely hours I could not be convinced
The tunnel even had a light
Wandering alone in the dark
Through the labyrinth of life
Waiting for a spark
To find the "one" who was right
Wanting to give up
But never losing up my fight
Running out of luck
Until you came into sight
Cautiously exploring
The possibilities of love
Without ignoring
Signs from up above
You intrigue my mind
With passion from the past
I'm hoping to find
A friendship that will last
Let fate decide
What next transpires
My heart is open wide
In anticipation and desire
My dreams will be sweet
With your hand in mine
Until we do meet
Mystery sublime

One

One sky
One moon
One sun
One earth

One life
One son
One choice
We are from
Who we are within

We are one
Connected to all

One within
Through each other
Earth, air
Fire, water

Karma returns
Energy collected
Body that burns
Soul resurrected
It all begins
And ends
With one

Authors Comments:
*"I wrote this while staying at Camelot Castle in Tintagel UK….. It was a moment when
I felt my strongest, connected to the world. And I can't wait to go back there someday"*

Without

It is without effort
I became your friend
It is without doubt
And without end

A world of change
Without fear
Love remains
The path is clear

Listen to the wind
Taste the salt in the sea
Take my hand
Let your spirit be free

Focus your energy
On possibilities
Without expectations
Without guilt or blame

Take responsibility
For your own actions
Nothing ventured
Nothing gained

Live in this moment
Without the past
Without the pain
Love in the present

Love
Unconditionally
For who people are
Not what you want them to be

Respect yourself
And the choices you have made
Without remorse or regret
What you don't like........ change

Meditate on ideas
Center thoughts in your mind
Leave your vibrations clear
To accept love divine

Tackle each challenge
Without any objection
Energy is a sponge
Keep positive interactions

Authors Comments:
"When you change the way you look at things, the things you look at will change."

New Love

Fresh new love
Full of possibilities
Time spent hanging out
Getting to know compatibilities
Hours lost talking
About life's mysteries
Smiling, flirting and laughing
At the idiosyncrasies
In sharing myself with someone new
I see a clear reflection
Of all that I've been through
Pointing me in this direction
Karmic energy
That brought us to this time and place
Magnetic synchronicity
Cosmic forces beyond the human race
Sweet coincidences
Melting past into present
Spirit and body dances
Kissing you in this moment
Hope long given up
On joining with another heart
Down on my luck
You've given me a new start
Frozen in fear
Afraid I'll screw it up
Holidays are here
It would be nice to be loved
I called upon a friend
To share the good news
And ear I did bend
With details and clues
Confirming my intuition
Nothing standing in the way
Confusing emotions

Not knowing what to say
Confident in my decision
To take a leap of faith
Give into the passion
God it feels great
Quick prayer to a higher power
For the gift of another chance
Couldn't wait to tell my daughter
I've begun a new romance

Can I Get Any Closer

Can I get any closer
To God than I am
I am one with mother nature
It's all part of the plan

My bottoms firmly planted
Into the ground
I am deeply connected
To this balanced I've found

Can I get any closer
To love than I am
No fear of the future
Devotion without demands

With my arms and heart open
The love is free to flow
A spirit no longer broken
When I learned to let go

Can I get any closer
To peace then I am
When I trust in the power
I hold in my hand

Earth, air, fire, water
Sun, moon and stars
Bring my spirit together
Heal all my scars

Can I get any closer
To you than I am
We are one within each other
I finally understand

We have a purpose
To create miracles
To spread joy and happiness
To overcome all obstacles

We are all created equal
Life is spiritual
Fear has no value
ANYTHING is possible

Silent Conversation

So much freedom in letting go
Undeniable pleasure
Watching love grow
From the pain of departure

So much emotion
In the palm of your hand
Love and devotion
Some do not comprehend

I feel the passion
Your need and desire
As you control your emotions
To maintain your power

So much heat
From a body so strong
Together complete
Apart for too long

Kind, gentle spirit
Sometimes fragile and weak
Commanding magic
No need to speak

Sweet soul's communication
Energy transferred
No need for explanation
Apology was heard

Forgiveness granted
Guilt removed
Another seed is planted
With patience and love

The silent conversation
Continues
Therapeutic exploration
Resumes

As the cycle slowly advances
To reconnect the circle
Without realities pretenses
To strengthen the oracle

Like A Rock

I don't know when it happened
I don't know where we went wrong
It just happened all of a sudden
It was there, now it's gone

Although we both still care
Something isn't there
And it's tearing us apart
Further than we already are

Neither side is pushing too hard
For fear of what they will find
Could it be that love is gone
Or are there just other things on our minds

I know that the love seems strong
But it's fading out inside
Has it been too long
How long can we go on

Our love is like a rock
You can throw it into the ocean
But it will not drown
Washed up on the shore
Is where it can be found
Ready to try once more

Perfect Mate

I'm beginning to wonder if there is any such thing
As a perfect mate
In the same breath I ponder to myself
How long am I supposed to wait

If he is out there, why can't I find him?
Where is he hiding?
Come out, come out wherever you are
I am right here waiting
Now I realize I'm not searching
Night and day
But I have been looking
Hoping love will come my way

I'm trying to keep the faith
Through disastrous dates and celibacy
Trying to believe
There's someone somewhere searching for me
Busy days, lonely nights
Aching to play
Am I supposed to settle
For the next one that comes along
And exist in social contentment
Sell out and admit my theory was wrong

Love is like the lottery
If you don't play
You will never win
Investing everything you've got
Only to possibly lose again

The Pieces That Fit

I found every man I ever wanted
In the arms of the man I hold
The friend to be honest with
The little boy I can scold
The man I have blind faith in
To take care of me when I am old

The father with his wisdom
And admiring eyes
The partner with the freedom
To fantasize

The lover who is loyal
Attentive and deep
The spiritual warrior
Who guards me in my sleep

The puppy I can play with
The squirrel I can chase
The man I'm going to spend my life with
Who keeps a smile on my face

The talkative girlfriend
With all the best gossip
My precocious politician
Who doesn't take no shit

The boyfriend that pampers me
And buys me special treats
The massage therapist
With a fetish for my feet

Kisses that melt
Explore and satisfy
Love that is felt
Stars that collide

The protector of my secrets
The inquisitor of my soul
My favorite pet
Especially when he licks the bowl

The teacher who expands my mind
The lover that stretches my body's limits
The mentor that encourages me to find
The pieces that fit

Same

Same ocean
Different shore
Waves of connection
Beg for more
Same Moon
Different rotation
Love blooms
In a distant location
Same infinite sky
Rain falls, sun shines
Arms question why
You are not in mine
Same stars
Different orbit
Near or far
You are with me in spirit
Same constellations
Different positions
Same expectations
Different perception
Same air
Different viscosity
Same care
Different ferocity
Same passion
Different hearts
Same intentions
Friendship starts

ONLY YOU

Only you hold the key
To our own destiny

Only you can be sure
What your future will be

Set your spirits high
Keep your feet on the ground
Don't say goodbye
If the love is still around

Take it one day at a time
Wait patiently
The change you hope to find
Maybe difficult to see

If you believe in your emotions
If love is still deep in your soul

Don't let the confusion
Make you lose control

Only you hold the key
To your own destiny

Authors comments:
*"This was written for my children. It is difficult to teach our kids
in this age of instant gratification how to manipulate their own
satisfaction; to create the world they want to live in."*

Let It Be

Let it go   Let it be
Give it love   Set it free
It's beautiful to see
When the love comes back to me
A circle bathed in light
Birth   Love   Life
Sweet innocence
Mature to common sense
I will always be amazed
By your skill   your style   your grace
Your curious precocious ways
That put a smile on my face
A little bit of trust
A smidgen of faith
Independence is a must
No, you can never be replaced
Nothing satisfies
My spirit or my mind
Than the look in your eyes
When it's time to go inside
Let it go   Let it be
Give it love said it free
It's beautiful to see
When the love comes back to me

Authors Comments:
*"If you set it free and it returns, it is meant to be; if it does not return,
be grateful you had the strength to set it free to be happy"*

Choices Broken Down

Life's choices always seem
To break down into two themes
Love or money
Pain or pleasure
Poetic fantasy
Or realistic future
Right or wrong
Smart or dumb
Opinions formed
From what we become
High or low
Doomed or lucky
Wealthy or broke
Now or someday
To be or not to be
Poignant question
Imprisoned or free
Faith or religion
Politically correct
Or socially outcast
Pay or collect
Either way you are taxed
So which investments
Are you willing to risk
Which commitments
Survive the loyalty test
Rise or fall
Grow or die
None or all
Live or die
Choices broken down
Reality or living dreams
Feet on the ground
Or chasing rainbows and moonbeams

Oh Friend; Oh Lover

Oh friend; oh lover
Can you coexist with each other
Provide strength when I am weak
Stand firm in your own beliefs
When my opinion speaks
No silence or intimidation
No eggshells to avoid
Intimate conversations
Without the lover becoming annoyed
No angry confrontations
When we don't agree
No need for solutions
Just enjoy the company
Can I lean on the friend
With thoughts, fears and doubts
If the demons come again
Will the friend help work it out
Without condemning actions
Or thinking of themselves
Will the lover act in frustration
Demanding something else
Can the lover forget
The daily trials and tribulations of the friend
Get lost in the moment
Where satisfaction has no end
To become consumed in the passion
In a touch or kiss
Overwhelmed with emotion
Would the friend get jealous

Oh friend; oh lover
Can you be separate from one another
Can the friend truly understand
The complexities of love
The simple touch of a hand
What it means, what it does
Without ever having melted
Body, spirit, heart and soul
Without feeling rejected
Or needing to control
Can the lover comprehend
Intensity that is never enough
With no signals from the friend
How will love know when to be gentle; when to be rough
Without the friend's communication
The lover is left to guess
So the answer to myself imposed question
If definitely YES
They happily coexist

No False Pretense

There is no false pretense
My intentions are pure
Words real and intense
With passion and allure
Not meant to break hearts
Or insight hopeless illusions
New friendships start
Based on mutual connection
Here I am skin and flesh
A human example
Available mistress
A world to sample
No hidden doors or trick wires
What you see is what you get
No resume required
Just honesty and respect
So give love freely
As I return the favor
Unconditionally
Each friendship to savor
To be sure that my hands
Are warm and gentle
Let go and understand
The soul is a temple
Karma unfolds
Fate is eluded
In the confusion
Alone and secluded
This is my confession

Life in Balance

The more balanced I get inside
More beautiful I become
The higher my spirit flies
The more powerful and strong
My exterior beauty
Is only a reflection
Of what is inside of me
The more I live my convictions
With faith and commitment
The more profound my passion
For creating sacred magic
So when I walk by
And people stop and stare
No more do I wonder why
I know what is there
The grin on my face
Is more than confidence
There's nothing left to chase
I am complete in lifes experience
I am invincible within my devotion
To allow miracles to replace
Fear and doubts confusion
I learned was simple hidden grace
I now stand tall and proud
Accepting only one truth that lasts
Living in the here and now
Allows my heart to trust
So beauty can be embraced
By all who choose to look within
Pain from the past can be erased
New life in balance can begin

Sometimes Lost

Sometimes: no matter what is going on
You feel lost and alone
Wonder where you belong
The chaos surrounds you
Deadlines and demands
Moments are few
Anyone understands

Choices and options
Who to let down
Priorities and prisons
Keep your feet on the ground
Sometimes our decisions
Affect those we know
Who share in our passion
Who to let go

Solid emotions
High and low
Strength of convictions
Or let weakness show
Trust intuitions
Then follow your dreams
You'll find satisfaction
If you truly believe

All Who Ache

So in this world of war and refuge
Where does reality lie
There's a line one must choose
But no one need know why

Comfort comes
To all who ache
Tired bones
Life mistakes

Hearts remain open
With shudders closed
Always hoping
For loves repose

Faith is never to be forgotten
Trust shall be earned
Spirits never to be broken
A friend's true concern

How

How is it done, two become one
And they share a life together
Years pass them by
They keep each other alive
The love between them
Just grows stronger
How do they stay together that way?
I will always wonder
What makes them hold on
When something goes wrong
How do they use their pain to get closer
Are they as happy today
As they were yesterday
When life seemed so much simpler
No babies to bathe, no homework wars
No pictures to save from the refrigerator door
No meals to prepare in 15 minutes or less
No signs that say beware, no psychological tests
No fighting over the phone, no chores, no stress
They use to come home
To a house that wasn't a mess
Now they walk hand in hand
Without remorse or regret
For what might have been
If they had never met
How do they get through
So many things
And keep their love new
With every challenge that life brings
It must have something to do
With the friendship they share
A love that is true
And the rings that they wear
How can it be
It's never happened to me
It's hard to believe
In a love I can't see
I once had a dream
Of living like that

Reality came
Slapped me on the back
How can I impart
On my children's hearts
The Glory of love
A good example I am not
Faith and trust
Hope and prayer
When the "me" turns to "us"
You're almost there
I envy those with the courage
To continue in bliss

Authors Comments:
"This is dedicated to Rick and Robin Santos after going to their 25th wedding anniversary party. I am in awe of people celebrating 25 to 50 years of marriage and I congratulate their perseverance and courage to continue"

Zoofactory Buffet

As I sit at my breakfast table
I am the fortunate witness
To an elegant theatrical miracle
And I know I am blessed

What a beautiful ballet
Of chaos and grace
A crowded soiree
Enjoying a feast

I supply the yard and the food
They reward me with a ravishing display
Of love, trust and gratitude
Here at the zoofactory buffet

As they chatter and screech
With joy and with glee
They innocently teach
Life's simplicity

What an exquisite orchestra
As the sun rises and sets
Sensational shapes, sounds and colors
Sublime silhouettes

In spring they dance in twos
A phenomenal cirque du Soleil
As the playfully choose
A partner for life's cabaret

The most amazing tango
Of fun and survival
Audio .... visual
A magical musical

When they settle down
At the end of the day
They know peace can be found
They have a safe place to live and to play

Times like these, I thank God I am around
To observe and take care of
My zoofactory

Authors Comments:
"One of my favorite things to do is to watch the squirrels and the birds, the bunnies and the dogs in the morning or in the afternoon. They never cease to amaze me."

If I Tell You That I Love You

If I tell you that I love you
I really mean the words I say
And if I tell you that I missed you
It means I thought of you today

The love that burns inside me
Is deeper than you'll ever know
There is a power that goes through me
When you let your love show

When you laugh, I laugh along
And when you cry, I wonder what is wrong
When you are confused, or think you don't belong
Just remember that I love you

I will love you forever
You're part of my heart and soul
An angel sent from heaven
To make our family whole

So if I tell you that I love you
It comes from deep inside
My love is unconditional
And my heart is filled with pride

Authors Comments:
*"This was written for my son, Christopher Shaw Griffin as a lullaby
so he knew when he was young how much he meant to me."*

Half

The power of your spirit
Led me into my backyard
I took a few deep breaths along the way
I looked around, then glanced back at my home
I felt a tug at my arm
Pointing to the moon
Halfway from being new
Halfway from being full
Kind of how I feel when I am not with you
Half lost in this life
Half grounded and in control
Half yearning to be a wife
Half loving the power to let go
Yet freedom has its price
Independence is not a goal
To love would sure be nice
But reality is cruel
I keep one hand in the past
To remind me of where I've been
If life is just a test
At least I know where I am
I'm half locked in this world
Half knows where I belong
Half a fragile little girl
One half a woman brave and strong
I'm staring at the moon
Through naked branches on the trees
Hoping you come stand with me soon
Bringing your half to me

Loves Cryptic Meaning

Love is just a word
Overused by some
Losing all it's worth
When it is given to everyone
Love should be given freely
To all that we meet
But spoken discreetly
To make the heart skip a beat
You can love a friend
You can love an object
The message you send
Is in how you project
When whispered
Love can lead to passion
Soft moans of pleasure
Intense sensations
When simply stated
In polite conversation
To one who waited
With anticipation
Words created
Loves consumption
When spoken intimately
Followed by your name
This word simply
Will never be the same
Yes, love is just a word
With limitless intentions
Cryptic meanings
Leading to infinite emotions

Invoking My Muse

If I could invoke my muse
It wouldn't be hard to choose
I would call upon the moon
Send a message through the runes
Chant a balancing tune
So I'd be ready for you
I'd warm my skin
With the power of the sun
Purified from within
No obstacles to overcome
Then I'd wait for the wind
To feel your gentle touch
Aching to begin
The dance I miss so much
Tease my senses
Bend my body to your will
Spirit dances
Let the mind remain still
Caress my breast
With a brisk breeze
Sweet tenderness
This moment I seize
Eyes closed
Breathe deep and slow
Comfort zone
Only my muse would know
Peaceful dismissal
Soul satisfied
Connection successful
Body energized
Contentment continues
Till I can look into your eyes

The Circles Come Around

In our most intimate interactions
While whispering in each other's ears
We challenge personal passions
While questioning our fears
We strengthen the emotions
That confirms our beliefs
Proving the power of our convictions
After years of counterfeiting thieves
The most simplistic concepts
Given to interpretation
Lest we ever forget
Our maniacal fascinations
There is no intimidation
Intelligence or influence
That cannot feed an action
Toward our spiritual romance
A lifetime of trust
Rewarded and wasted
An existence of lust
True love yet untasted
Now with eyes wide open
And true love within our reach
I yearn to hear the words spoken
I ache to feel your touch
Soft lips that move
As I drink in the sound
Nothing left to prove
The circles come around

Love Does Exist

I believe in the abundance
That the universe has to offer
I believe in the romance
And so I found the perfect lover
I trip once in awhile
Over my fear and doubt
Then I see your smile
I just want to shout
Love does exist
In the here and now
I hear your promises
And I believe you somehow
I get back on my feet
Down the broken path
To where love and happiness meet
And I know my own worth
Doesn't matter how I look
Where I live or what I drive
I'm still writing my book
I know what it means to be alive
You saved me from the past
Who I may have been
Time flies so fast
Yet here I am
I believe in creating your own destiny
Working towards a goal
Having faith that what is meant to be, will be
In this life I want to hold your hand
Be your partner and your friend
I believe you are the only man
Who will stand by me till the end

Everything

If I had to tell you in one word
What your love meant to my world
EVERYTHING
If I thought of all the things you do
To make me think of you
EVERYTHING
How can you be everything
When I can't think of anything
BUT YOU

Will you settle for perfection
In the here and now
No expectations
Of tomorrow

Just mutual satisfaction
Of how this love feels
Complete overwhelming passion
Love that is real

No doubts or hesitations
Of what this is
Raw, honest emotions
Pure intimate bliss

I will hold you forever
Believing you are the one
Living happily together
With no fear of what's to come

I will invest every ounce
Of time and energy
In making an "us"
Out of the you and me

Treasure every moment
I have you in my arms
Miss you every second
You're not here to keep me warm

It amazes me how everything
Reminds me of our love
It surprises me that in my fantasies
You are still "the one"

If I had to tell you in one word
What your love meant to my world
EVERYTHING
If I thought of all the things you do
To make me think of you
EVERYTHING
How can you be everything
When I can't think of anything
BUT YOU

Authors Comments:

"Love when it surrounds us is intoxicating........ And from that feeling we emanate more love, making it stronger and pulling it closer....... Love can be amazing"

Treasure Box

I have a treasure box
I keep in my mind
There is no need for a lock
It is there for all to find

No mystery, no secret key
Just pieces of my past
That have molded me
Easy access, for all who choose to see

Everything I have become
Every failure, pain and test
All my hidden wisdom
Is there to be blessed

Deep within my eyes
And the wrinkles on my skin
Years of love and smiles
Wealth beyond reason

My treasure box is full
Of my children's laughter
Images come to view
Of my proud mother

Cards made with crayons
Puppet shows and pets
Kisses by the millions
There is nothing my heart forgets

The gifts and the giggles
Accumulated over time
The silent struggles
To balance my mind

Vivid pictures
Flash up on my screen
Infinite treasures
To be saved and seen

There is plenty of room left
In my treasure chest
For more stuff
For future quests

Each day I am grateful
For the treasures I've been given
I am so thankful
For this life I am living

Authors Comments:

"This was a challenge to come up with a concept of what would I put in a treasure chest to save to be opened after my death. I found that my most treasured things are the memories I keep within, not the things I own. My children would be happy if I got rid of a lot of my stuff, but it reminds me of these moments that I treasure."

Greener Grass

When the grass looks greener
On the other side
Of a fence that's higher
Than your spirit can fly
Look a little closer
And ask yourself why
Do you think it's better
In someone else's life

Do they have more love?
Do they have more faith?
Do they have more stuff?
Do they have more strength?

You think you work harder
Not a doubt in your mind
You deserve a bigger
Piece of the pie
You're not getting younger
Your spirit is tired
It doesn't seem to matter
How hard you try
You feel "life" is passing you by

What is it that you envy
That you think you see
In that perfect house or family
Is it so far fetched
For you to believe
On the other side of the fence
They wonder the same thing
When the grass looks greener
On the other side
Of a fence that's higher
Than your spirit can fly
Dig a little deeper
Look beyond your pride
It may be human nature
But cast your judgments aside

Give them all your wisdom
Give them all your trust
Give them all your support
Give them all your love

If we all work together
The grass will grow
The fences will disappear
The next generation will know
We have the power within
Peace
Can be here and now

Authors Comments:
"I have always believed that we reap what we sow.
For every seed that is planted another tree will grow."

My Baby

For nine months
I carried you around
Never realizing
How sweet you would sound
Never quite convinced
You would ever arrive
Until I saw your face
When you first opened your eyes

I never felt so much joy or love
So much pride or pain
A gift from above
Life will never be the same
With you laying in my arms
I never felt so needed
By anyone before

You've given me a family
And so much more
Just know that I love you
From your first breath to your last
From your overwhelmed mother
To the daughter I never thought I would have

Authors Comments:
"This was written on the day my daughter; Samantha Lynn Griffin was born 27 years ago. All her life she has inspired me, infuriated me and loved me despite my flaws. She is my angel"

I Refuse

I will not allow my intuition
To affect the smile on my face
I refuse to have expectations
I know infatuations are easily replaced

I will not let doubt cloud my vision
Or sabotage my fantasies
I refuse to lose my motivation
Or sacrifice my dreams

I will not let logic control my emotions
Or take away my faith
I refuse to rationalize my passion
Or admit love could be a thief

I will not give in to temptation
Or lose myself in loves ideals
I refuse to accept obsession
I refuse to kneel

I will not become neurotic
I take life as it comes
I enjoy being "lovesick"
I refuse to run

Letters

I keep writing letters
That I never plan to send
Poetry is much better
When a heart is trying to mend

These thoughts die with me
What do I leave instead
Words written on paper
For you to read when I am dead

Stories of pain and agony
Of love and loss
Journals from history
Years of therapy to toss

Explanations
To all the questions
You've been asking
All these years
Can only be answered
When I am no longer here

So I leave this legacy
Of truths unknown
To your discrepancy
When you are grown
I loved deep
I fell hard
Do not weep
I'm finally a star

Complete

I feel better when I hold you in a tight embrace
I melt with a look
When you put your hand on the side of my face

I ache for your sweet kisses
That set my body on fire
The way your tongue tells me secrets
Of your burning desire

There's a safety in your arms
When fear and doubt take control
Like a protective alarm
That listens to my soul

You hear every word I do NOT speak
You keep me strong when I feel weak

You challenge my intellect
Without making me feel dumb
You give me love and respect
Knowing where I come from

You stretch my spiritual concepts
To a higher more powerful realm
This love we share is infinite
In your arms it feels like home

You pay attention
And act accordingly
You smother me with affection
But never suffocate me
You come to me, even when I do not call
Playfully, you distract me from my hell
Instinctively you know
If I start to fall

And in my heart I know you will catch me
You were not meant to save me
Just to complement me
Thank you for loving me

Authors Comments:
"There is only one man who makes me feel complete and he knows who he is"

I Want to Believe

I want to believe
What I see
When I look deep
Into your eyes

I want to believe
I'm the only one
Who ever made you
This comfortable, this alive

I want to believe
I'm special
You can't live without me
That love is unconditional
That I fulfill
All your fantasies

I want to believe
No one else
Has touched you like me
Or quenched your appetite
Or kept you satisfied

But I know better
I am just another body
To keep you distracted
And occupied

I want to believe
In miracles
That broken hearts
Really do heal
So I can return
Too trusting what I see and feel

I want to believe
In the words that I hear
When you whisper them
Passionately in my ear
That you will always
Be here

God I want to believe
That forever could exist
That love is real
And you are the one
That I waited for this

To be wrapped
In your arms
So content to fit so tight
Hand in hand
Bodies entwined
As we sleep through the night

Yes, I want to believe

My Soul Cries for You

If I made a profession
Of this unconditional love
I have had in my possession
All of my life, since I was born
Would you accept my apology
For not seeing in your eyes
Everything I ever needed
To succeed and survive
I covered my heart with fear
Lack of wisdom and trust
The pain and suffering of many years
Buried in broken promises and empty lust
You've always been there
Spirit to guide
Gentle touch always near
Patiently waiting to be led inside
When I am tired and lost
Lonely and consumed
I feel the strength of your love
Quietly pushing me to move on
My soul cries for you
In the dark of the night
With every stage of the moon
No longer needing to wait
To be bright and full
Again I tempt fate
As I am calling you, I'm ready to invest
With mutual intention
On our infinite quest
To resume intimate attentions
No more excuses, or higher priorities
No fear of consequences or insecurities

Lose Yourself

Lose yourself in me
In my eyes
In my touch
Lose yourself in the passion
In the fire
In the love
I stand naked before you
No trepidation
No regret
I surrender to you
No walls
No pride
Lose yourself in this gift
In its beauty
In its light
Lose yourself in the comfort
In the peace
In the calm
Lose yourself inside me
Gentle rushes
Soft and warm
So that I may vanish too
Mind, body and soul united
No longer are we two

Watching Me Grow Old

I see the sympathy
In your eyes
As you watch me
Slowly die

I feel the compassion
In your voice
The contention
Of this choice

I see the reflection
The loyalty
The dedication
The history

I see the sadness
On your face
At my loss
Of dignity and grace

I feel the affection
When you hold my hand
Your emotions
I understand

I know your worries
They were once mine
Always in a hurry
Racing against time

I sense your fear
Of what the future holds
When you visit me here
In this crowded home

I feel the sorrow
Of your soul
Watching
Me
Grow
Old

Authors Comments:
"This was written for my grandmother, Ruth Shaw when she was in a nursing home....... It was hard to watch her deteriorate and slowly die"

Oh This Life

Get up in the morning; put the kids on the bus
Grab a quick cup of tea, now I'm in a rush
Race down the freeway with the top rolled down
To get to work in another town
Put in my time, collect my check
The car is speeding with my mind
I don't need another ticket
Pull into the drive, unlock the door
Walk the dog who peed on the floor

Oh this life
Seems to be consuming me
A mother not a wife
Footloose and fancy free
Barely enough time
To eat, sleep and breathe
Oh this life is consuming me
Kids return home smiling
Tell me about their day
Papers, pictures, assorted things
Memories for us to save
An hour to relax, the kids watch TV
I work in the yard or read a book
About everything that is wrong with me

Oh this life
Cub scouts, brownies, soccer games
And people wonder why I am insane
Doctors, dentists, PTA
I wouldn't have it any other way

Showers are taken, teeth are brushed
Read a book, no more need to rush
Quietly talk before a lullaby
Time for my babies to sleep, so their spirits can fly

Oh this life
Dishes are done, clothes clean in the drawers
Pets are fed, who could ask for any more
I lay here in bed, pen in my hand
Collecting my thoughts, trying to understand

Oh this life
Seems to be consuming me
I'm so proud of myself
I do it happily
Content in my own little world
With my family of three

Authors Comments:
"This was written for my angels who are grown and gone now, what I wouldn't give to go back to this way of life now. I do get some of this from my granddaughter, Sophia Marie Griffin, when I watch her and it brings back fond memories"

What Magic Brings

How'd I get so lucky
To find my everything
After years of being lonely
See what magic brings

Sometimes I think
It's just too good to be true
Every time I blink
There you are with something new

Another way to show
Your love for me
The passion grows
So easily

A whispered word
In the middle of the night
The energy transferred
In a kiss after a fight

That little grin
That shows your dimples
When I let you win
Love is so simple

Sometimes I fear
I'll awaken from this dream
You won't be here
To spend your life with me

Then I get a tap
From the little boy
With a one track mind
Being oh so coy

This little girl loves to play
Tease and flirt through the day
I have to smile real wide and laugh out loud
Shake my head and roll my eyes
But my baby knows I'm proud

To call you mine
You're still my favorite playmate
My lover and best friend
The one I think of when I wake
The one I want to hold at each day's end

How'd I get so lucky
To find my everything
Could it be
Time to stop running?

Awaken

Awaken your feelings
Open your heart
Find out what's inside yourself
I know it may seem hard
It's time to be honest
About what's in your soul
To me and to yourself
Let me in or let me go
The stones are charged with emotion
Both good and bad, no secret love potion
Just thoughts that I've had
I need to be true to who I've become
I won't lie and say the love is gone
I won't try to get you back
I know it's been too long
But I think it's time to end the game
It's time to be brave and strong
Maybe we can still be friends
If you open your eyes
Then awaken your heart
Think of new beginnings instead of ends
Think of the future and where to start
Stop letting the logic rule
When your instincts know the way
Awaken your heart and soul
Accept what they feel and say
No matter what you see
A life with her or me
A child is still your responsibility
Awaken your mind to see
He needs you as much as he needs me

I Watch

I watch you walk
I watch you play
I see you brace yourself
For every step you take
I listen as you talk
Of things you remember
Of things you forget
Such pride I feel
In your every move
A love so strong
Not even death can remove
Age has done wonders
The wisdom shows in your eyes
Each wrinkle tells a story
So it should come as no surprise
How much you are admired
For your beauty and your strength
How deep inside we all desire
To be like you someday
As you go through each day
Being thankful you're alive
Know the important role you've played
In a family that struggles to survive
The influence you have had
On so many hearts and minds
Is the legacy you've shared
To be passed down in our family throughout time

Authors Comments:
*"My grandmother and my mother were matriarchs in
every sense of the word. I wrote this for them"*

You Have Given Me Hope

You have given me hope
When I had none
You untied the noose rope
Took away the proverbial gun

You have filled me
With love and light
Honest integrity
You gave me back my sight

It will never be easy
But I'm trying to believe
My perception is rusty
But I know what I need

I know how I feel
When you are deep inside
Desires that are real
I am unable to hide

There are truths that you know
After only a week
That have never been told
Guarded secrets that I keep

You have broken records
And destructive patterns
A look without words
Makes my body yearn

You have surpassed
Every test
At the top of a class
Full of misfits
From a tortured past

Mind warns "too fast"
You're already missed
You just left
And I'm feeling this

I don't care about logic
Or cynical precautions
I know you fit
Without hesitation

I hold you to no promises
I make no comparisons
I long for your kisses
Your touch and your passion

You are too good to be true
But I am trying to trust
While I miss you
I am no longer lost

I've Never

I've never imagined love could be so beautiful
Until I saw it through your eyes
I never believed in fairy tales
Till I got you as my prize

You shared with me your innocence
Taught me how to trust
Unconditional love without pretense
Knowing love cannot be lost

I've never loved stronger
Never gone deeper
Never felt younger
Never been weaker

It's hard to watch you struggle
As you try to balance life
When all I want to do is cuddle
Tell you everything will be alright

You have the keys to my soul
Hidden up your sleeve
I don't want to let you go
But I know you want to leave

I keep holding onto the amazing memories
Years flashing through my mind
Sweet, delicious fantasies
Of silence and solitude

Now I find
Nothing seems to satisfy
Like the comfort of rewind
Going back to fortify
Images lost in time

Echoes of lullabies
Forgotten and left behind
I know you won't go far
Still too much to share

Flying to a star
Just to get some air
No matter where you are
Close your eyes
I will be there

Authors Comments:
*"Written for my children Chris and Sam..... As a parent we invest
so much into our children only to watch them walk away"*

Without A Mother's Love

Without a mother's love
Where would children be
Without a mother's strength
Who would sustain the family

Without a mother's understanding
Where would children turn
Without a mother's guidance
How would children learn

Without a mother's embrace
Children would not know ecstasy
Without a mother's smiling face
Children would not know security

Without a mother's gentle touch
Compassion would disappear
Love wouldn't mean too much
If children lived in fear

Without a mother's vision
How would children see the light
Without a mother's passion
How would children know when to fight

Without a mother's patience
Children would not know creativity
Without a mother's innocence
Children would not know fantasy

It takes a mother's intuition
To know when something's wrong
A mother's love has no conditions
It simply exists for her children

Children rarely comprehend the comfort
That lies in a mother's arms
Until the day comes
That a mother is gone

Every day should be a celebration
Of all the things a mother does
Moments of reflection
A lifetime of love

Authors Comments:
"Everyone has a mother, some better than others. My mother was amazing and now that she is gone and I miss her every day, this poem just means so much more. I have always tried to be the best mom I could be for my kids. Being a mother has been my greatest challenge and my biggest success."

Your Wings

Oh my adorably sweet
Baby angel butterfly
Time to leave your fears and your feet
On the ground .... It's time to fly

You are ready
I can see it in your eyes
Slow and steady
All you have to do is try

Stretch those wings
Build a firm foundation
Carefully with strings
To ease your trepidation

Give shape to a picture
Of who you want to be
Visualize the future
It will become what you see

Angels white wings
Innocent yet mature
Mischievous sprite who sings
Intelligent and demure

You are being released
From a lifelong cocoon trapped within
Safe in the family womb
As your adult journey begins

Look again in the mirror
To see the beauty you've become
These doubts can make you stronger
There is no need to run

Wings are made to fly
Above the rocks and land
Over the oceans that divide
You no longer need to stand

Magnificent butterfly
Intense and agile
It's time to say goodbye
To the weak little girl

Celebrate your wings
Your wisdom and your talents
You can do ANYTHING
You're an angel who is radiant
No matter what the future brings
You are ready to be independent

Authors Comments:
"Dedicated to my baby number one, Samantha"

Worth Chasing

You intrigue me
With the possibilities
You sound so sweet
New loves mysteries
Anticipation
Of what could be
Exhilaration
Mixed with fantasy
Like a dream
That wakes you up
Breathing heavy
In a puddle of sweat
With a smile on your face
And a sigh in your heart
As your body shakes
Knowing what you want
Your eyes open
To the light of day
Spirit has spoken
Time to play
Yawn and stretch
Grin still unbroken
Mirrors catch
Cheerful reflection
Amazing energy
Thoughts racing
This could be
Worth chasing

Let Us All

Let us all
Take a moment to remember and rejoice in life today
Take a moment to be grateful for every breath that you take
Take a moment to understand he would want it that way
Take a moment to recall all the love he gave
Let us all
Take a moment to overcome our grief
Take a moment to give praise for the memories we keep
Take a moment to surrender to the tears and the pain
Take a moment to remember the smile on his face
Let us all
Take a moment to honor a man we respected and loved
Take a moment to thank the "father" for leaving her with us
Take a moment to listen to the birds sing of spring
Take a moment to remember every little thing
Let us all
Take a moment today and for the rest of our lives
To appreciate our loved ones while they're still alive
Take a moment today to write a letter to a friend
For the support they give, pray it never ends
Take a moment today to listen to the wind
Absorb the wisdom his spirit still sends
Take a moment today to call the woman who survives
Because no matter what you pay, not to call is a higher price

Authors Comments:
*"This was written in honor of my grandfather, Marshall Albert Shaw,
for his funeral and to remind us all to treasure the gift of life"*

Assessment

We have so much more
Than we need to survive
So many things we take for granted
Too much envy .... Too much pride
We abuse all our human rights
What do we really need
To live a happy life
We need faith to believe
We need to walk in the light
We are where we need
To be at this time
So open your heart and breathe
We have nothing except time
It's not money
It's not what you drive
Or where you live
It's in your eyes
How you look at the world
How you react
How much have you learned
How much have you given back
Next time you assess
Things you've achieved
Don't count your assets
Count how you believe

Authors Comments:
"Too often we forget how the things we nurture affect all those we touch."

Love Will Find a Way

There is an incredible peace
Deep within your eyes
A look on your face
When you release a tiny noise
That heavy sigh
That follows a content moan
Or the tear in my eye
When you say, "you're not alone"
The tingle down your spine
With a gentle caress
The grin when I mimic, "mine, mine, mine, mine"
Followed by a passionate kiss
There is intensity
To every touch or hug
A genuine sincerity
When we make love
There is a strength in your embrace
A powerful energy
That exceeds time and space
When you're holding me
There is a comfort when we cuddle
That defies explanation
A look so subtle
It requires rumination
There's a definite force
Pulling us closer every day
For better or worse
Love will find a way

Cravings

We hold so many doors open
While we try to find the right path
Words too often spoken
When the actions didn't match

So we test the waters
Wading just above the knees
Of different lovers
Hoping our heart sees

A rainbow or a light
A reflection of love
A reason to fight
To find the strength to rise above

The power of a conviction
A touch that gives chills
An intense passion
That defies free will

The intoxication
That makes us crave
A simple connection
A memory to save

That urge to swim
Beyond reality
The power within
Serendipitous intensity

Motivation to move mountains
To conquer the world   .
Without hesitation
To go for the gold

The impulsive obsession
That pushes beyond the comfort zone
The mad fascination
That always leads us home

After you swim in the ocean
With the defiant undertow
Life's little predilections
Allow energy to flow

We learn to ride the waves
And crash against the shore
Until the body craves
Just a little bit more

Poetic Illusion

I took a chance on love
After years of isolation
Down under and above
All illogical emotions
Sweet adventure
Spontaneous acts
Intuitions that capture
Deception from facts
Smiles forgotten
Long lost passion
Heart is smitten
Poetic illusion
Opportunity grasped
With no regrets
Love has passed
Spirit doesn't forget
No expectations
Interest fades
Different convictions
Choices made
Broken but not beaten
Investment retrieved
Soul survives lesson
I still believe
I am worthy of
Time and energy
Someday true love
Will find me

Find the Love Within the Hate

Find the love within the hate
And the pain you will escape
Find sincere gratitude
Behind that negative attitude
That made you feel weak and used

Find the strength to send love
To those who betray you
Find the courage to rise above
And your sorrows will be few

Do not suffer in silence
Forgiveness is the key
Release your need for justice
To the powers that be

Take solace in the circumstances
And gifts of this moment
Especially with second chances
Timing is vitally important

Do not rush to find answers
When questions consume the heart
Let love fill your senses
When bodies are apart

Stay true to your convictions
Be faithful and honest
Listen to your intuition
When it comes to love and trust

Don't take communication for granted
Work hard toward your dreams
Nurture the seeds you planted
Give others what you need

Allow yourself to break
So you can become stronger
Give more then you take
Know love always conquers

Fear produces failure
To run away is the biggest mistake
With love work together
Forever is at stake

Authors Comments:
"Sometimes it is easier to be angry and hate the world for the things that have happened in your life and the people who have exacerbated your misery, but in reality love is the only truth that can set you free"

A Soul Never Forgets

My love follows your soul
Wherever it may go
I will not lose my self control
Or try to explain things you already know

I will not break down
And try to communicate
For I have found
It is easy to love; hard to hate

In my silence you will learn
What I knew once as fate
These tables have been turned
And I know it's too late

I realize these words
Have been spoken before
But I never understood
The pain that comes, when you ask for more

No anger
No regrets
A memory can erase
What a soul never forgets

Blind Faith

It's not in the logic
It's all in the love
Some call it magic
A gift from above

A powerful feeling
A spark to a flame
A spiritual healing
That echoes your name

It's not in the logic
It's all in your heart
A strength in the music
Makes the fire start

Emotions run rampant
Out of control
Possibilities are infinite
When you connect body and soul

It's not in the logic
It's all in your dreams
Close your eyes you can see it
You need only to believe

I Am Your Northern Star

Our love is more than unconditional
It is infinitely elliptical
Made up of many intertwined circles
Dependent on one another's cycles

We will never be over

Like the moon that must wax and wane
We are doomed to evolve and change
The sun that must dawn and set each day
Is the constant anchor in reality

We're destined to become more than a fantasy

I am your northern star
As you have always been mine
I see better in the dark
You see best when I shine

We are the perfect complement to the others detriment

You are the earth   I am the ground
I am the air   You are the wind
You are the fire   I am the flame
I am the water   You are the waves

We epitomize the magic of two connected spirits

When our bodies are not together
The love does not stop
The passion grows stronger
While we heal our individual hearts

Only when we're both balanced, can love conquer all

There's an intense power; a knowledge and a faith
We belong together and magically all pain is erased
Wants and needs combined into an unforgettable kiss
Universe has defined our love is bliss

Fantasy and reality become one and there is no need to run

Together we will find a way to dismiss
The demons of our minds, I promise you this
Forever is the only goal
Heart, mind, body and soul

You and only you can make my dreams come true

Authors Comments:
*"I am always surprised that with every relationship I have had in my life,
I always tried to believe in forever. My heart was always
convinced that this would be the "one".*

This is Thanksgiving

A day to be thankful
A time to stop rushing
The beginning of the season to be grateful
A day to give a little deeper praise
For the miracles in our lives
A child; a job; a raise
A gift; a smile; a compromise
We give thanks for the things we own
Or wishes that have been granted
We give thanks for love that's shown
Or guidance a higher power has provided
We give thanks for our families
Our pets and our friends
We give thanks for the memories
And true love that never ends
We give thanks for our healthy children
The joy that they bring
We give thanks for the laughter
That can cure anything
Every day I am grateful
For lifes tiny details
To be hopeful; to be helpful
To breathe deep, then exhale
Some people are not as lucky as I have been
I'd like to take a silent moment
Thinking about them
I extend my deepest sympathy
And healing energy
To those who have lost a loved one
That cannot be here today
They are here in spirit
Watching over the festivities
I hear them in the quiet
I feel their presence constantly
I pray for
People less fortunate
In need or in pain; lost or alone
Just existing to complain
Without the benefit of a happy home

Or a supportive family to sustain
I consider myself blessed
In so many ways
I am grateful for the past
That has led us to today
I give thanks for the connections
And the love that is shared
In the simple interactions
A holiday meal purposely prepared
With love and devotion
To all the people that are here
Thank you for being part of a tradition
And I hope to see you all next year

Authors Comments:
*"This was obviously written for a thanksgiving meal to remind all who
sat at that table how grateful I am to have them in my life"*

Prayer Answered

I never thought I would believe
In happily ever after
Too many times, I've been deceived
So I stopped hoping for forever

I gave up on love
I gave up on trust
I gave up on life
My spirit was lost

Just when I thought
I couldn't take any more
An angel was sent
To answer my silent prayer

I have to admit
It wasn't love that first sight
But there was an incredible comfort
That my soul couldn't fight

This angel disguised
As a simple man
Took my heart by surprise
When he held out his hand

There was something in those deep blue eyes
When I caught a glimpse of them
Staring into mine
I looked away but could not deny
A passion that is hard to find

This quiet gentle soul
Wanted more than I was looking for
But he slept so sweet and peaceful
The attraction needed to be explored

Not playmate material by his own submission
He wanted a monogamous commitment
Intrigued by his suggestion
He became permanent

This was no epic fairy tale
Where the prince gets to rescue the damsel
Unless you consider the financial peril
Then I could say, "you saved the day"

You my love
Saved my soul from sinking
Into an abyss of dark and cold
The emptiness of the unfeeling
I no longer know

Your incredible patience
Won you the biggest prize
The gift I never shared in any romance
Was given to you with trust and pride

Authors Comments:
"Sometimes it is when you least expect it to but need help most, that love shows up on your doorstep. This is dedicated to my angel David Allen Miller"

In the Moment When I Surrender

In the moment when I surrender to the passion
Time stands still and your kiss becomes my obsession
I have free will
But I cannot move or breathe
As your fire begins to slowly consume me
I fall into your arms as your lips explore
You hold me strong
As I beg for more
You feel my heat
Admit defeat
My spirit will devour your soul
If you have the courage to let yourself go

Warrior

Has my warrior weakened
From too many years at war
Has he given in
To existence, giving up demanding more
Is his silent discontent
Enough to conjure the warrior princess
Shall I leave him to suffer his malfeasance
Or torture him with visions of what he missed
His armor is tarnished but intact
As he hunts for answers and solutions
Testing theories and facts
Ignoring his neglected passions
In his deliberate solitude
He cultivates his spirit
Realizing the magnitude
His actions have had on it
Picking up his sword
He assumes a battle stance
His faith dependent on every word
He cuts the ties that hold him hostage
Alone he stands
Proud and determined
The princess takes his hand
Knowing trust has been earned
Together they can battle any demon
Or natural real world force
A new kind of freedom
A new life course

"WE"

In these fragile moments
Of despair and destruction
We find the inner strength
To examine the dysfunction

Lost in a haze
Of busy realities
Existing day to day
Instead of "living" the dream

Caught in a cycle
Balance and focus disappear
Both become unstable
Consumed by doubt and fear

Spiritual connection
Begins to fade
Habitual reactions
Demand the love is saved

Separate to find solutions
Be strong despite the desolation
Fighting through the commotion
Silently aching for compassion

Finding individual convictions
Within the concept of a "we"
Filtering through the confusion
Of what we each want that to be

Love finds faith and forgiveness
In honest repentant eyes
A powerful awareness
The truth of temporary goodbyes

Trust begins to return with verification
Two hearts no longer concerned with explanations
There is magic in the kisses full of passion
There is hope for reconciliation

Forever doesn't seem so far
When you live in this moment
Together we can step out of the dark
Into the light of our rejoined spirits

Authors Comments:
"Sometimes love needs a break or separation to realize how important it is. Sometimes it leads us back to love, sometimes it does not."

Will You Be Mine

It was more of a feeling
Than a state of mind
More of the believing
That I was different inside
Now I look at myself
As being plain
So I took today
To look again

I found a lady
I've never seen before
Who knows what she wants
Yet still asks for more
No longer a dreamer
No longer strong
A simple believer
That life must go on

Vulnerable to feelings
I've never known
So much in love
Yet just learning how to let go
I guess I'm still growing
I don't ever want to stop
I want to grow closer
Not further apart

It's hard for me to change
The way I've always been
Insecure and alone
Just trying to win
In this game of life
I've been thrown in

I'm happy now just lying in your arms
Listening to your heartbeat
Spending time alone
I think of our love and I feel different
I feel special
And loved

I think now I come to the end of the line
Time to look to the future
It is there that I find
The question to the answer
"Will you be mine?"
I'm speaking of marriage
A good deal of hard work
A total commitment
To the one I love
A lifetime spent
Making our dreams come true
My only dream now
Is to grow old with you

WHO

Who have I affected? How??
Who have I touched?
Who have I rejected? Why??
Who have I loved?

Who in my life has changed who I am?
For better? Or worse?
Have I also changed them?

Who has motivated me
To pursue my dreams
Who has influenced me to see
The truth is what you believe

Who has molded my mind
To grow; learn and expand
What do I seek to find
When I try to understand

Who has given me inspiration
Who has broadened my horizons
Have I infected people with my passions
Or do they see twisted manipulations

Who has taken the time
To guide me in the right direction
Without leading me down a path
Of self pity or self destruction

Who has touched my heart
Without trying to steal a piece of my soul
Who anticipates what I want
And never considers control

Who has made me contemplate
The mysteries of the world
Made me question love and hate
Who has always protected the little girl

What have I accomplished
When, where, how and why
To satisfy someone else's wishes
When I laugh until I cried

Who has attempted to manipulate
With anger, jealousy and fear
Who instigates my comfort and my tears
In the silence I create
The energy that keeps love near
This is a tribute to appreciate
All those who care

Authors Comments:
*"I have always questioned everything in life.
This poem reflects some of those thoughts"*

I Love Your Ways

I love the way you look
Your boyish little grin
The way we talk
About everything and nothin

I love the way your blue eyes shine
When you like what you see
When you say, "mine, mine, mine"
And you're looking right at me

I love the way you're generous
Honest and trustworthy
And that you seem oblivious
When mushoo is with me

I love the way you make me wiggle
And keep me wanting more
You have a devilish a little giggle
And the fact that you don't snore

I love the way you're patient
With my cycles and moods
I love every little moment
I get to spend with you

I love your arms wrapped around me
The way you touch my cheek with your hand
I have fallen hopelessly
For a "simple man"

I love the way your shoulder muscles flex
When you're on top of me
And I know what's next
When I can't hear you breathe

I love the ear to ear smile you get
When the puddles get so deep
Everything gets wet
Then you fall to sleep

I love all the little things
And the big stuff too
Thank you for wearing my ring
I am forever grateful

You are my monkey
I am your bumblebee
We are both lucky
I'm so happy to be me

Authors Comments:
"This was written as a valentine's poem to my love David"

My Resurrection

I know who I am
I am proud
I understand
How hard
It is to be a man
To be allowed
To put head in hand
And cry out loud
I know where I belong
Naked in your arms
I know I am strong
I should be on the farm
You were wrong
To abandon me and run
But here I am
Creating my resurrection
Releasing the fear
Of failure and rejection
I will push the stone
Away from the passage
I am not alone
The angels have a message
I have been reborn
From the depressive ash
It is my turn
To prove love does exist
My power is restored
To a higher level of consciousness
The question now is yours
Are you ready for this????

Let Another Day Begin

Let the sun warm my face
As I lay in bed half awake
Nothing but a pillow to embrace
I try to find the courage
To tackle another day
Get past the pain and confusion
Create some magical illusion
That life is worth living
Love worth giving
Yet my heart feels empty
Hope lost somewhere along the way
Head hurts constantly
But the world doesn't wait
So I yawn and stretch
Let the transference begin
Allow the energy to flow
Letting the light enter my skin
Warm and peaceful
Bright and hopeful
I rise to the challenge
Before the clouds roll in
Delaying my awakening
Let another day begin

Authors Comments:
*"Sometimes you just don't have the energy to get out of bed but life
goes on and it must be done. Thank God for stubborn will."*

Running From Rainbows

On a journey through my mind
I took a detour by my soul
I was not surprised to find
She was alone and cold
I asked her "why do you stay this way?"
When you have so much to share
And so much to say
Why do you insist on pushing everyone away
They say my depression is an illness
I swear I have no control
Truth is I've grown to know the loneliness
That consumes and surrounds my soul
Maybe it's fear of being hurt again
It's so much easier to just pretend
I didn't count on you
To warm my heart and be my friend
I over react
You try to understand
When I'm about to crack
You simply hold my hand
You make everything better
You read me like Dr. Seuss
To everyone else I'm Shakespeare
To you …. It's a moose on the loose
I know there is no excuse
For the tragedies I introduce
You don't need the abuse
I'm just tying the noose
You say this is all so simple
Be merry, be happy, be gay
What we share is so special
I feel like a needle lost in the hay
You bring out the sunshine
I follow with the clouds
The rainbows we paint together
Would make De Vinci proud
We could chase it forever
Hoping to catch a glimpse
Of the beauty within its colors

Or walk away and call it quits
I need the passion
I don't know how to live without my pain
I crave the deep emotion
Only you can seem to tame
Forgive my reactions
While I learn to refrain
From running from the rainbows
To make a little rain

Mediaeval Dreams

I close my eyes and fall into the past
Shining knights slaying dragons
For damsels in distress
Mounted on white steeds
With honor and integrity
Forgoing their own needs
For a woman of virtue and beauty
Long golden hair
Soft silken skin
Seductive stare
Innocent grin
Feminine perfection
Tiny waist, busting bosom
Pouting glossy lips
Fainting for no reason
Men with character
Muscles and brawn
Lords and masters
Masculine and strong
Excellent lovers
Eager to please
Mediaeval musketeers
Sweet are these dreams

Authors Comments:
"For GER"

He Teases My Senses

There is a magic
To the way he touches me
In those sacred moments
Between awake and asleep
His gentle caresses
Gliding over my skin
His body presses
Melting me into him
He teases my senses
With soft sweet kisses
On the back of my neck
Making me wet
There is a barrier
That is penetrated
As he enters her
Love consummated
Wiggles and squirms
Whispers in my ears
Wrapped in his arms
Making love without fear
Flesh against flesh
Causes heavy breathing
Liquid rush
Kids have gone swimming
Intense emotions
Dreams become real
Love without questions
Perfect moments we steal

A Whisper of Power

I am the witch you've been looking for
I am all you require
Then a little bit more
I can fulfill your desires
With merely a phrase
A whisper of power
Will leave you listless for days

I am here in the dark
I am there in the glow
I am your favorite work
I am the sprite that you know

I do not doubt or question
The strength of our love
I have no expectations
I simply enjoy what I have

I am not jealous of the others
Or the life that you share
I envy your time together
Just breathing the same air
There is nothing better
Then your heart beating in my ear
And whenever you need me
I will be here

Breezes

I will try to be strong
For the both of us
I will leave you alone
But that's not what I want
I will send you my love
From a distance
I will speak to your soul
When the man will not listen

On hurricane winds
I will scream my desires
To hold you again
Feel the heat of your fire
With breezes that whisper
True love conquers all
I believe in forever
But I can't do it alone

Your spirit keeps calling
On each breeze that comes by
Save me I'm falling
Don't let this love die
It begs me to trust
To see past your fear
Emotional gusts
I can't help but hear
You've got to hold on
Baby please don't let go
I will leave you alone
But you need to know

I still have faith
In loves powers
The magic we've made
Over the years
You know we belong
With each other
The connection is strong
And I sure miss my lover
The passionate kisses
That make time disappear
The kitten who wishes
That her man was still here

I will try to be strong
For the both of us
I will leave you alone
But that's not what I want
I will send you my love
From a distance
I will speak to your soul
When the man will not listen
On hurricane winds
I will scream my desires
To hold you again
Feel the heat of your fire
With breezes that whisper
True love conquers all
I believe in forever
But I can't do it alone

My Amazing Angel

So what is wrong with me
How can this be love
I can't eat or sleep
There's no balance in my life

And then there is you
So perfectly peaceful
Happy to exist and view
The world as acceptable

Here I am
Not sleeping again
In pain and agony
As I try to hide my misery

Yet your patience soothes
Even my most horrific moods
Love is for fools
Yet here I am in love with you

Your grin erases
Doubt and anxiety
Your tolerance leaves traces
Of what I always dreamed love would be

Passionate and playful
Impressively loyal
Unbelievably unconditional
Determined and dependable

Intensely indomitable
Fantastically faithful
Spiritually powerful
Sexually insatiable

My incredible
Adorable
Amazing angel
I am a lucky girl

Thank you

Authors Comments:
"Dedicated to David"

Be Thankful

There are times in life
When you feel you have nothing to be thankful for
Though these times are few and far between
They do exist for us all
Times that everything takes too much energy
You just need time to breathe
Be thankful for that breath
When the lawn needs to be mowed, leaves raked, bushes trimmed
Be thankful that you have a house to live in
Times when the sink is full and the hampers overflowing
Be thankful that children are still around
Because they are quickly growing
They're always moments
When you want to escape family responsibilities
Take a minute now to fall on your knees
And thank God you have people to care for (that care for you)
There are times when the list of things to do
Becomes too long and gets neglected
You need to be thankful your body is capable
And get motivated
Times when you realize work consumes your day
Meditate; exercise…. then take time to say thank you
And be grateful that you have a job to help you pay your way
When you are alone and all is quiet, reflect on your blessings
As few as they may seem at times they do exist
In the simple, mundane activities of life
From washing the car to a child's hug and kiss
Without all the stress ….. think of all you would miss
If you take time to notice and be thankful
The stress goes away when you see the beauty around you
And thank God for another day

You Are My Moon

You are my moon
And my sun
My man
The one

I used to honor you
Adore you
Worship you
All you had to do
Was shine

You grounded me
From far away
The stars could see
How well we played

Even when you were gone
You were still there
Holding on
Illuminating my darkest fear

Keeping everything I knew
In balance in the universe
New or blue
You eliminate the curse

Allowing my theories to prove
Nothing is by chance
I am worthy of love
Just being who I am

Burning Bridges

I use alcohol to dull the senses
To numb the disappointment
To keep from facing consequences
Of lost and failed investments
Yet sadly nothing is modified
No matter how hard I try
I wake up with you still on my mind
Sometimes I just want to die
I search for strength
In mindful meditation
I'm relying on faith
To get me through this confusion
Bridges are being burned
With each path that is chosen
When will I learn
When my heart is hard and frozen
I stand alone
Watching this inferno
No escape known
No choice but to let go
With each inch I release
The pain cuts a little deeper
I wish for nothing more than peace
That love will keep us together
Ashes blowing in the wind
Charcoal fills the air
If I could do it all again
I would still want you here

Strong Enough

Am I strong enough to love you
And save you from yourself
I spent my whole life searching
For my other half

Now I am left alone to question
If this witchcraft is real
Can I make another potion
That will help my angel to heal

Is it fair to hold you
In moments stolen in between
When the demons haunt you
I taste your tears and feel your screams

We share the same essence
The same energy
You're the only one who gets it
You are my destiny

But am I strong enough to love you
Keep you safe from harm
When our moments are few
And the day is long

Are you strong enough to love me in return
And save me from myself
I am a self destructive woman
You know I need your help

How Can Love Be So Simple

How can love be so simple
Yet so complex
A certain grin and dimple
Or the way one bites their lips
The passion of a kiss
The heat of a touch
A look that tells what you miss
And just how much
The depth of the connection
That cannot be explained
The silent conversation
Or the hidden shame
Loves strength and frailties
Tested to the limits
Questioning fidelities
Never losing the magic
The intensity and power
When no words are spoken
Apart or together
Love is always forgiven
Unconditional
But not without limitations
The soul forever loyal
Waits for human recognition
Faith is now crucial
Let go to hold on
Love is not optional
You are the only one

Trade Math

Building a foundation
On the sands of trade
Destined for dysfunction
If changes are not made

Physical attraction
Does not hold
Sexual satisfaction
Trade gets old

Simple addition
Weighs what is fair
Empty emotions
Pretending to care

Desperate manipulation
As one heart bleeds
Guilts sadistic motivation
Usually succeeds

Subtract the complications
Of love and forever
Moments of passion
Minus all the drama

Innocent intentions
Financial needs
Controlling the situation
The hand that feeds

Easy multiplication
Time erodes all possibilities
Creating confusion
For future fantasies

Playful interactions
Now have a higher cost
Irrational expectations
Trade value is lost

Now to start with the division
Of time and energy
Sever the connection
Expediently

Working with the fractions
In the final days
Finding new distractions
To start another trade

Authors Comments:

"Sometimes we get caught in a catch twenty-two when we are in relationships that do not work the way they should. It's never easy to stay or to leave, nothing makes sense, so we start over and end up in the same kind of relationship all over again wondering what we are doing and how did we get to the same place. Eventually lesson is learned and we can start over fresh."

What Faith Drives Us

We're all victims of our pasts
Slaves to our futures
Consumption driven rats
In a hypocritical culture
Politically correct drones
Clones that do not differ
Idealism lost
Individuality suffers
Creativity is tossed into a pile
Of things that are not profitable
Defeated, we conform
Into what society calls "the norm"
Never believing that one person
Can change the world
Sending sacred souls off alone
To feel isolated and castrated
By their need to feel connected
Humiliated by the fact
They just never "fit in"
What keeps us going
When all hope is gone
What keeps us searching
For a place to call "home"
What strength from within
What force ………….. What light
What faith drives us
Through the days
Then through the nights

Could it be God
Could it be she
Could it be God
Could it be he
Or could it just be a desperate need
We all have to connect
Tired hearts that bleed
Living lives without respect
Cold and alone
We fight blindly through the storm
In hopes we might find
"THE ONE"
Dazed and confused
Feeling beaten and used
Watching those around us
Rape the world God gave us
Of its majesty and beauty
All for what?

Thinking out loud
Feeling humble yet proud
We wonder .... What can I do?
What difference can I make
What could I change
That could turn things around
What magic could I use
So that peace can be found
Change your point of view
Have faith in your love
It has to start somewhere

Why not with you???

Returning To Me

Once upon a time
I knew my strengths
And weaknesses
The power of my mind
My blessings
And my curses
Somewhere along my path
I got distracted
And deceived
I almost lost my faith
When love decided
Without warning to leave
I have taken time
To mourn
And to heal
Only to find
Death allows me to be reborn
Pain allows me to feel
Now I return
To a state of trust
And happiness
No longer concerned
About what I lost
Or what I miss
Hope is slowly growing
Through the patience and love
Of a beautiful soul
His actions are renewing
My convictions that love is enough
And true love does conquer all

I am stepping into a light
I used to embrace
As sacred
A way of thinking
A way of life
Negativity erased
No anger
No hatred
Simple positive energy
Given
And received
A man who loves me
And deep within
I know he will not leave

Authors Comments:

"I find it so easy to get caught up in other people's drama. I invest in myself till I feel strong and then someone comes along in need and sucks the life right out of me. I have tried to train my brain to focus on me, but inevitably it seems I always get caught up in opposing energy. This poem reminds me to keep fighting and believing in myself and the power of love."

The Magic of ME

I do not live in the past
But it has molded who I am
The ways that I react
The things I comprehend
When I am awake
The demons dare not roam
It is not until I sleep
That they take control
Trying to bring me down
So I feel their presence
And any balance I have found
Meets with great resistance
I am stronger now
I have risen from the ashes
The fire that burns below
Only represents my dominant defenses
I have always felt that with death
Comes the power to embrace life
When there's nothing to lose left
It's easier to make things right
I am an army within myself
I have conquered many battles
There's a lifetime of wealth
In a soul that will not settle
In the here and now
I know what I want
And who I want to be
I will make it work somehow
That is the magic of me

I Am Stereo

You think you live in black and white
But I see a lot of gray
You say you don't have the strength to fight
But you have the will to walk away
You tag me as destructive
Because I make you think
Your explanations are selective
Maybe you should have a drink
I am the Technicolor dream
High maintenance and high definition
A constant emotional stream
Of pain, pleasure and passion
There is monotone
Then there is me
Live on paper and in stereo
For the world to read and see
You are correct
I am not easy
I have intellect
And spirituality
I will question the universe
And all its inhabitants
Then I question what I am worth
To the viewing audience
I am REAL I am HERE
Just a girl with no fear
I embrace the challenge
Of living life amongst the stars
And dealing with the damage
Of being true to who we are

Triton's Rule

Violent waves crash against the shore
My spirit needs to ask
What is life for
To do nothing but invest
To be thrown to the floor
Another wave begins to crash
Another slamming door
What does the ocean expect
From the turbulent seas
Does Triton have regrets
From all the fishes he sets free
How can I find balance
When the waves crash so close
With no way to make sense
Of the things I love the most
I understand the anger and the fury
Of each crescendo wave
Another heart is buried
Another soul is saved
The water is calling
Summoning me to swim
The moon is begging
Me to try again
The sky is clearing
The rain starts to fade
My love is screaming
Walk away
Footsteps echo
In each puddle that I pass
Whispering let go
Leave it in the past
The wind is howling
Look up
Look to me
Close your eyes my child
I will help you see

There in the dark
On a cold rainy night
Faith makes me look up
A full moon encircled in light
Reaching out with hope
From my true love's hand
The truthful words you spoke
Guided me back toward the land
One final wave hits the rocks
Where my foot once rested
As if Triton himself
Came to pronounce
"Keep the faith"
"You have wisely invested"

Authors Comments:

"I wrote this one dark night when suicide was on my mind. At the beach where I often end up to think, I was overcome with defeat. If it were not for the wind and the waves whispering to me, I would not be here."

Edited

Eager anticipation
Of magical moments shared
Personal perfection
Of how someone should care

Evil expectations
Outline drawn
Creative limitations
Influenced by only one

Evolving illusion
Crayons on the table
Tempting artistic expression
From grave to cradle

Seeking satisfaction
Technicolor dreams
Mutual exploration
Examining beliefs

Excitable emotions
Feelings bruised
No explanation
Love is never refused

Simple confusion
Truths softly spoken
Momentary lapse of reason
Image adjusted, not broken

Subtle alterations
Expand perimeters
Ideal collaboration
Vision fused together

Exterior manipulations
Distract one from the other
Creating limitations
Draining both of power

Infinite alterations
Carefully fine tuned
With words and actions
Sun, stars and moon

Flowing with passion
Dangerous with a pen
Valuable lesson
Here and now; not then

New broader direction
Improvisational
Edited version
Now three dimensional

LEGACY

When you think of your parents aging or your children growing
What do you imagine
What do you want them to know
How do you want to be remembered
When it is time to let life go
What do you want to leave behind
When God decides that it's your time

Will you pass down your wisdom
Or your talent or your wit
Will you pass down your freedom
Or the strength of your spirit
What will you leave as your legacy
To let the world know you were here
What gifts have you bestowed upon your family
So they might find some comfort in their tears

What kind of memories
Will they have to embrace
Will they remember your beauty
Your style or your grace

Have you kept in contact with those you profess to love

Have you spoken words from the heart
That will echo in their souls
Have you share your ideas and thoughts
For your last wishes, dreams and goals

From the moment a child is born
We try to teach right from wrong
We provide food, clothes and a home
We try to improve their lives
From what we recall about our own

But what do we really leave
Love, pain, hate, anger
Sympathy, jealousy, greed
Patience, understanding, hope, honor
Empty pockets and promises
Prayers that they succeed where we failed

Bitter resentments .... Typical rivalry
Personal investments
In the future of the family
Too little too late
The opportunity has passed
I touched the hand of fate
The legacy gets lost

Authors Comments:
"I am plagued with thoughts of death quite often. And I question what will happen when I am no longer here. Hoping that my legacy is clear all I want is to be loved in death as I was or am in life"

Wiggle

It started with a wiggle
A smile, and then a giggle
Now I've got your attention
Maybe I should mention
I've been watching you
From across the room
And damn boy you look good
Do you think you could
Move a little closer
Put your hands on my hips
We can move together
To the sound of the music

Something like this

Try a little circle
Now let's pick up the speed
Make the circle bigger
Keeping rhythm with the beat
And then I start to wiggle
To the left and to the right
Followed by a smile
And a giggle of delight
See I told you this was easy
Something else is hard
Our bodies fit perfectly
Dancing in the crowd
If you turn me around
I can look into your eyes
Baby don't stop now
You're doing just fine

I Am the One

I am the one
Still patiently
Waiting for
THE ONE
I am the one
Still blindly
Praying
For love to come
I am the one
Still quietly
Crying
All alone
I am the one
Still honestly
Hoping
Dreams come true
I am the one
Still openly
Smiling
When I am blue
I am the one
Still truthfully
Wondering
What to do
I am the one
Still secretly
Wishing
It was you

Angel Wings

There is an angel
Lying next to me
Cuddled up close
Sleeping peacefully

An angel in a body
Naked and warm
Next to me
In perfect physical form

I listen to his breathing
Melodic and serene
I get this blissful feeling
Like I'm living in a dream

Every now and then
This angel's wings
Begin to extend
Beyond imaginings

Certain I will be here
Waiting patiently
He flies without fear
Confidently

Always he pays attention
To be sure I am in sight
With love and compassion
He holds me through the night

Free to leave
He chooses to stay
Helping me to believe
Not everyone runs away

I am so grateful
For the love
Of this angel
Who makes me feel special

I hope he understands
The importance of his influence
This angel .... This simple man
Has given me a second chance

Authors Comments:
"For David"

Full Moons Mist

On a waxing day
Just before the moon is full
I find the need to play
I choose you
Under the sheets
I ache for true loves touch
I call your spirit to me
To participate or watch
As my hands find spots
Only secret lovers know
I send the pleasure off
In search of you
I grin at the thought
You will soon awake
Sweaty and erect
No it was not a mistake
As a write
My body is naked
Only candles
Light the room
My hair is wet
My body is soft
My love is sent off to you
I tease myself
As I know you would tease me
A cool breeze
Caresses my body
Tantalizing the nipple
You have claimed as your own
When I rock back and forth
My playfulness is shown
A drip of cold water falls
From the tip of my wet hair
Slowly making its way
Down my skin
Like your tongue
To you know where
Holding off
On letting go

Making sure
You are aware
Little pleasures
So often missed
Delightful treasures
I send to you
In the full moons mist

Authors Comments:
"Only the spirit of true love can elicit such magic"

I Pledge My Allegiance

I pledge my allegiance
To no one but you
Upon my honor and my countenance
I shall remain true

Be thee inside me
In my blood, flowing through my veins
Consumed by your energy
Love will never be the same

Power known only
To those who choose to see
The passion and focus
When you are within me

Courage beyond comprehension
As fear disappears
You are my complimentary extension
Without you, I would not be here

Beauty that commands attention
Wisdom beyond my years
Total satisfaction
When you are near

Hear me clearly
As I profess my intentions
Watch as my veracity
Tests my confidence and convictions

Faith that knows no boundaries
Love without conditions
Balance becomes easy
Together we are perfection

So this day I vow my loyalty
From now into eternity
To live in complete harmony
And allow you to love me

Authors Comments:
"Do not be misled by this poetic illusion. The love of which I speak, is not human. But the intense expression of being connected to the spirit within and the energy of the universe."

Printed in the United States
By Bookmasters